cial Media and Mental Health
Handbook for Teens

BY DR CLAIRE EDWARDS

THE AUTHOR

Claire Edwards (BSc (Hons), PG Cert, PsychD, PG Dip) Clinical Psychologist based in London. She first began king in child and adolescent mental health services in 1 and has been working as a clinical psychologist since qualifying in 2008.

re has worked with families in a variety of settings, working with individuals, parents / carers, families, groups and schools, assessing and treating the mental health and behavioural difficulties that children and adolescents present with.

Claire has had a longstanding interest in the broader factors which impact the lives of young people and their families and a passion for enhancing family relationships.

Claire is also a parent, so she also has a personal interest in the wider influences on families and how they affect relationships.

First published in Great Britain 2018 by Trigger

The Foundation Centre
Navigation House, 48 Millgate, Newark
Nottinghamshire NG24 4TS UK

www.triggerpublishing.com

British Library Cataloguing in Publication Data

A CIP catalogue record for this book is available upon
request from the British Library

ISBN: 978-1-911246-37-4

This book is also available in the following e-Book formats:

MOBI: 978-1-911246-40-4
EPUB: 978-1-911246-38-1
PDF: 978-1-911246-39-8

This book is also available to purchase as a bundle with our
Social Media and Mental Health Handbook for Parents and Teachers :)
BUNDLE: 978-1-912478-25-5

Cover design and typeset by Fusion Graphic Design Ltd

Printed and bound in Great Britain by Clays Ltd, Elcograf S.p.A

Paper from responsible sources

www.triggerpublishing.com

Thank you for purchasing this book.
You are making an incredible difference.

Proceeds from all Trigger books go directly to
The Shaw Mind Foundation, a global charity that
focuses entirely on mental health. To find out more
about The Shaw Mind Foundation, visit
www.shawmindfoundation.org

MISSION STATEMENT

Our goal is to make help and support available for every
single person in society, from all walks of life. We will
never stop offering hope. These are our promises.

Trigger and The Shaw Mind Foundation

CONTENTS

Introduction. 7

Chapter 1: What's Out There? 10

Chapter 2: The Positives of Social Media. 27

Chapter 3: The Darker Side of the Internet 32

Chapter 4: How To Manage Your Internet Use 52

Chapter 5: Am I Internet Savvy. 69

Chapter 6: Have a Conversation 76

References 80

Useful Websites 84

CONTENTS

Introduction

Chapter 1.

Chapter 2.

Chapter 3.

Chapter 4.

Chapter 5.

Chapter 6.

Epilogue

Bibliography

INTRODUCTION

The internet is a complex and exciting world – one that you might visit every day of your life. You are in the first generation to be completely involved in the digital culture from birth, in a way that most adults in your life weren't. Social media is most likely a very normal part of your everyday life, and if it isn't, it might be quite soon.

Your generation is often talked about as "digital natives"[1] – that means you've grown up in this world of the internet and social media. The adults in your life, on the other hand, are "digital immigrants"[2], born before the everyday use of digital technologies. So some parts of social media are foreign to them, and they might have a harder time understanding all the things you take for granted about the digital world.

This can sometimes make adults around you cautious, because they're trying to support you and help you to use something safely while still learning how to get to grips with it themselves. This is where this book, and the book for parents and teachers, can help you.

It's totally understandable if adults are worried about how you will get on with the internet. It is developing so rapidly that it can be hard to keep up! You might find moving your way through the online world a little tricky. How should you manage criticism or bullying online, how do you know if you're spending too much time on the internet, do you understand the risks and how do you know if you are keeping yourself safe?

Bit by bit we are learning about the impact of the rapid rise of the internet and social media on young people, and researchers are trying to keep up with this fast-paced world. There's lots of different pieces of advice out there from lots of different people, and it can be hard to know where to start and who to trust.

The internet was started for researchers to connect with each other in the 1960s. By the 1970s technology had improved and by the 1980s people were getting computers at home. After this, the internet became more business focused. In the late 1980s, messaging systems began being used in groups and privately, which was the stage before social networking as we know it now.

One of the biggest shifts has been the change from web 1.0 to web 2.0. Web 1.0 was all about content – you went to a website and read its information, but you couldn't interact with anyone. Web 2.0 is all about communication – you can chat / play with other people, make online communities and change the content of websites. All of this was developed for adults and not with children in mind, which means that you are online in an adult setting, often without any support. The internet also changes quickly, so it can be hard to keep up with the latest websites and apps and ways of doing things.

Some young people (and indeed adults!) can find it hard to know how to behave online. As humans we are driven to make relationships with others, and the internet is just another way of doing this. But just like life offline, these relationships online can be complicated and you will need to think about how you manage yourself and how you respond to others.

The other major change has been the introduction of smartphones and tablets. Much more portable than laptops and personal computers, these devices can be used anywhere, anytime. Even the way we watch television has now changed. With digital television, streaming services and the internet, we can now watch programmes whenever we like! Back in the day children's TV programmes were only on at certain times in the day and there were only a few channels. Can you imagine!

This book exists to help you navigate yourself online safely and allow you to protect your mental wellbeing in a preventative way. It is based on my therapeutic work with families, along with research and current recommendations. For some of you the online world might feel unfamiliar, and for others it's just a completely normal way of life. And so, as with everything, there will be parts of this book that will fit for you, and other parts that won't. You'll take away what is useful for you, and I hope that it will help you think about how to keep yourself safe and happy within the digital world.

76%
of teenagers in the US use at least 1 social media site.
(AAP, 2016)

CHAPTER 1

WHAT'S OUT THERE?

In 2016, 23% of children aged 8–11 and 72% of children aged 12–15 in the UK had a social media profile. That's a big number for such young people.

Not only that, but this number doubled to 21–43% for children who are 10 and 11 years old, and increased to 50–74% between 12 and 13-year-olds.[3]

When you consider that children and young people are using social media in the evening (a tenth of 11 to 15-year-olds are still communicating via social media at 10.00pm[4]) and using likes and shares as a form of social currency, these websites are having a huge impact on young people in terms of their sleeping habits and identity formation.

While the internet is fast-paced and changes really quickly, it is important to have some knowledge about what is on the internet and why your parents or carers might have some worries about the apps and websites you're accessing. Below are some of the concerns that your parents might have about the most popular types of app, social networking site or websites used today.

WHAT TYPES OF SOCIAL MEDIA, APPS AND WEBSITES ARE MOST POPULAR WITH CHILDREN AND YOUNG PEOPLE?

Video Streaming Sites

As you'll probably know, video streaming sites and apps – the most notable, at present, being YouTube – are incredibly popular right now, especially among people of your age. Videos can provide a wealth of information, entertainment and knowledge, and can open up whole new worlds for people, without them ever having to leave their homes.

EXAMPLE:

YouTube

YouTube allows users to upload videos of their own and watch videos posted by other users across the globe. Their mission is "to give everyone a voice and show them the world. The platform is used by people who can set up their own accounts for free. They can post videos, watch other videos without signing up for an account, and develop a huge online following. Businesses also use the app in order to advertise and promote themselves.

YouTube is fantastic because it acts as a great platform for budding actors, directors, musicians, editors, and many other young people who want to learn new skills. It's also a fabulous alternative to the TV you have at home.

DID YOU KNOW?

Older children prefer using YouTube to watching content on the TV.

In a report by Ofcom, when asked whether they prefer watching YouTube or watching TV programmes on a TV set, 42% of 8 to 11-year-olds and 41% of 12 to 15-year-olds said they were much more likely to opt for YouTube.

CONCERNS

Why might my parent or carer be worried about my use of video streaming sites?

The challenge for YouTube – along with other social media sites – is the speed at which they can detect and remove inappropriate content or activity, given the huge amount of material uploaded daily.

- The potential for children to stumble across sexual or age-inappropriate content. Parents and carers are often concerned that their young children will easily be able to stumble upon this kind of material, even when they aren't actively searching for it.

- The risk of being exposed to disturbing, violent or traumatising material, which can have bad effects on your mental health.

- Copyright infringement.

- Revenge porn.

- "Related content" suggestions, leading children towards unwanted videos without them realising.

- Children becoming exposed to potentially unsuitable commercial advertising

- Privacy issues, lack of understanding of terms and conditions, and difficulties in monitoring your use.

TIPS FOR USING VIDEO STREAMING APPS SAFELY:

- Take the time to read through the app's terms and conditions thoroughly.
- Check the minimum age restrictions and make sure that you're not using any app or website while underage.
- Take advantage of the filters on video apps and websites, if there are any. On YouTube, for example, you can go to settings, tick "safe search filtering" and tick "strict". Check Google or the site's FAQ page to find out how to navigate this on other sites.
- Be careful about what you click onto.

Social Networking Sites

There is a huge array of social networking apps, websites and platforms that allow users to set up their own public or private profile, on which they can share photos, information, and updates about their day-to-day lives. Social networking sites are a fantastic way of staying in touch with friends, and they're especially useful for keeping in contact with people who live a long way away. They're also great for hosting and sharing news stories and inviting your friends to events!

EXAMPLES INCLUDE:

Facebook

Facebook is a popular social media website developed by Mark Zuckerberg when he was a student at Harvard University. In order to use it you need to set up a profile, which asks for information about you. "Friends" are then added to your page via requests, which you can accept or deny. You can post status updates, upload photos and videos, and comment and like other people's statuses.

Businesses can create pages and use them to promote themselves, using a basic free page or paying to advertise services. People can also use the platform to create groups and event pages.

Users can set privacy settings so that only "friends" can see their entire page and have access to their photos, or allow open access so that anyone is able to view it.

DID YOU KNOW?

Facebook has an enormous following. Ofcom (2016) reported that 43% of 8 to 11-year-olds and 52% of 12 to 15-year-olds were most likely to consider Facebook their main social media profile. In October 2012, Facebook had one billion monthly users, and in July 2017 it announced it had doubled to two billion monthly users [5]. That's over a quarter of the world's population using Facebook!

A rapid rise in user numbers is the reason for ongoing concerns about how Facebook is able to monitor and moderate the content posted on its site. In the past there have been some difficulties in getting distressing or offensive content taken down from the platform. Some recent shocking examples of this include footage from the US; one video involved a 14-year-old live streaming her own suicide, while another showed someone shooting and killing an elderly man. Facebook announced in May 2017 that they were employing an additional 3,000 workers to moderate content.

In recent years, Facebook has also come under considerable pressure and criticism for its handling of users' private data.

Twitter

Launched in 2006, Twitter is a website that enables users to publish short messages ("tweets") of up to 280 characters. Users "follow" other users (and therefore become "followers") in order to see these updates. Unless a user changes their privacy settings, anyone can follow a particular person's profile. Users can retweet or quote other people and leave their own tweets in reply.

CONCERNS

Social networking sites come with their own risks and potential dangers that your parent or carer might be worried about. These include:

- People's data being shared without their consent, even by verified apps.

- Users accepting terms and conditions without reading them and understanding what they're agreeing to.

- Oversharing of personal and private information without thought for the consequences.

- Trolling, where certain people are targeted and attacked either by strangers or people they know.

- "Witch hunting", in which people are subjected to public shaming or harassment for something they may or may not have done.

- "Fake news" – sharing of information that is not verified, has no source, or is simply untrue.

- People sharing fake news or fake accusations without corroboration.

- People stealing photographs or other people's information without consent.
- "Hacking" – someone using someone else's profile to ruin their reputation or access their private data.
- Targeted advertising.
- Cyberbullying.

TIPS FOR SAFELY MANAGING YOUR USE OF SOCIAL MEDIA NETWORKING SITES:

- Make an agreement with your parent or carer as to whether they can follow your profile to make sure you're safe.
- Check the minimum age restriction and make sure that you are not underage.
- Be careful not to share private information.
- Don't leave your Facebook or other account logged in so that other people can access it.
- Set up passwords on devices so that they can't be accessed if left unattended.
- Check your privacy settings and make sure that only people you know can see your photos, information and updates.
- Consider changing your settings so that you can decide what photos you are tagged in.
- Remember that whatever you put online affects your safety and online reputation. **Think twice** and **carefully consider** everything you post before you post it.

- Make sure you know how to report concerns and block inappropriate content. Sites should have FAQ pages that will provide you with this information.
- For advice on Facebook hacking, visit www.facebook.com/hacked.
- Be careful about what you click onto.

Photo Apps and Websites

Apps and platforms on which people can post photos of themselves, their friends and their lives are incredibly popular, especially among children and young people. Some of the most popular types of photos that people post on these apps are "selfies", which are photos that individuals take of themselves.

EXAMPLE:

Instagram

Instagram is a website designed for posting and sharing photos with friends via an app on your smartphone or device. There are ways to enhance, edit and alter photos, such as using filters to make them appear brighter or more aged, like an old Polaroid photo, for instance. Instagram is a great tool for fostering creativity and inspiring budding photographers and filmmakers. Friends can tag each other in their photos and, just like with Twitter, they can use hashtags in order to be found more easily online. Just like on Twitter, you gather "followers" on Instagram, and gathering a higher following can become very important to some people. Interestingly, Instagram was acquired by Facebook in 2012, along with some other social media apps and platforms.

DID YOU KNOW?

The Children's Commissioner[6] tested young people's understanding of the terms of conditions of Instagram. 56% of 12 to 15-year-olds and 43% of 8 to 11-year-olds in 2017 had an Instagram account, so it is important to explore young people's understanding of their rights in relation to social media. The terms and conditions for use were 17 pages long, 5,000 words in length and used sentence structure that only a postgraduate could be expected to understand!

The young people involved begged to stop when they had only got through half the text, because they felt that they couldn't understand it. As with most social media sites, the report highlights that young people must understand that "you waive fundamental privacy; the app could track you even when not in use; your personal data could be bought and sold; the terms could change at any time without notice, and the app could terminate your account as its sole discretion."

Ofcom asked a law firm to write the terms and conditions in a simpler way which the young people could engage with and understand. Their ideas about using Instagram changed once they were more informed and understood their rights. One young person even deleted their account as a result.

CONCERNS

Understandably, any platform that allows children and young people to share photos publicly can cause unease for parents and carers. Some worries include:

- Instagram and similar apps can result in a lack of privacy.

- Children and young people are often unaware of their personal rights and rules around copyright.

- Users can often have their photos stolen and used elsewhere online without their knowledge or consent.

- Instagram and other photo apps may contribute to people feeling FOMO – a fear of missing out.

- Photo editing apps and software can lead children and young people to believe that the "perfect" or "ideal" images they see online are real, and therefore they will feel inadequate and self-conscious as a result.

TIPS FOR MANAGING YOUR USE OF PHOTO APPS:

- Make sure that you understand the risks of using photo apps, such as a lack of privacy.

- Consider making your photos private rather than public. Remember that if your profile is public, your teachers, friends, family and future employers can see your posts – especially as they can leave a digital footprint even when deleted.

- Use the blocking and reporting functions if you are attacked online or made to feel uncomfortable.

- Bear in mind that a lot of photos online are edited, and therefore they often present a false representation of reality.

- Talk to your parent or carer about your confidence, self-esteem and body image if you're worried that your mental health is being affected.

Messaging Apps

There are a huge variety of messaging apps available for free, and they are particularly popular with children and young people. For teenagers especially, staying in touch with friends in incredibly important, and messaging apps provide a free and fun way to do so.

EXAMPLES INCLUDE:

Snapchat

Snapchat is a photo or video sharing app, on which any content that is shared is time sensitive. A picture can only be viewed for a few seconds before it disappears. If a screenshot is taken of the image, then the user is alerted. Users can now also add to their "stories", feeds that last for just 24 hours before disappearing. Some people aspire to get the longest Snapchat streak, which is when users send each other direct snaps without missing a day. Snapchat streaks can become quite addictive because users are "rewarded" with emojis (small illustrative icons often used in text and online messaging) when they reach certain milestones.

There has been recent controversy around this app, which added another feature – Snap Maps – of which many users were unaware. This is a feature which enables users to see exactly where their friends are and what they are doing. You can also view videos and / or photos of strangers who are posting from popular events or locations. The app needs to be changed to "ghost mode" in order for data not to be shared. Many parents, carers and even children were, understandably, upset because they hadn't been made aware of this breach of privacy, one which holds significant safety risks for young people.

WhatsApp

WhatsApp is an instant messaging service which can be used on smartphones, tablets and desktops. It works a little bit like text messaging. There's no cost to message friends, as it uses an internet connection. You can use it for one-on-one conversations or set up a group, and it can be used to share messages, images, and videos. You can also use voice messages and make telephone calls. Users can update their status to let other users know whether or not they are available.

WhatsApp was acquired by Facebook in 2014. It attracted controversy in 2016 when it announced that it would start sharing account information with Facebook, and users had to ensure their privacy settings did not consent to this if they didn't want it to happen.

CONCERNS

While the opportunity to easily message friends and family is a positive thing, parents and carers do have some worries about messaging apps, including the following:

- The prevalence of cyberbullying on messaging apps, especially on Snapchat, where offensive posts can disappear.

- The potential for data breaches and risks.

- Location services making children and young people easy to locate and track down.

- The risk of grooming and sexual exploitation of children online.

TIPS FOR MANAGING YOUR USE OF MESSAGING APPS:

- Check your privacy settings and make sure you're happy with them.

- Be vigilant and bear in mind the risk of cyberbullying and grooming (more on this in "The Darker Side of the Internet" chapter).

- Be mindful of who you're talking to and what kind of information you're giving them.

Blogging Sites

While the sharing of visual content such as videos and photos becomes ever more popular, there are still a lot of children and young people who write and create blogs ("web logs", writing that discusses a wide range of topics, including food, fandoms, hobbies, lifestyle, gaming and beauty). There are many blog hosting sites out there that allow users to host their blogs for free.

Blogging is a brilliant way for budding young writers, journalists, and photographers to build on their skills and foster their creativity.

EXAMPLE:

Tumblr

Tumblr is a social networking and microblogging (small blogs consisting of a few sentences) site. Users have a "dashboard" which allows them to see a live feed of the blogs they follow, which they can like, comment on and repost. Users can also connect their account to other sites such as Facebook and Twitter, so posting on Tumblr would then automatically send a tweet and / or Facebook post. It was set up in 2007 and acquired by Yahoo in 2013.

Tumblr has been criticised for its adult content (most notably pornography) and also for hosting content glorifying or depicting self-harm, suicide, and eating disorders. In 2012, Tumblr changed its policy and banned content that promoted these issues with links to support organisations provided.

CONCERNS

Your parent or carer might have the following worries about blogging sites:

- The risk of young people accessing inappropriate content, such as pornography, misogyny, discrimination, racism, or posts glamorising self-harm and eating disorders.

- Exposure to negative comments and trolling.

- Lack of privacy or risk of oversharing information.

TIPS FOR MANAGING YOUR USE OF BLOGGING SITES:

- Be mindful of the fact that you could potentially access harmful content.

- If you come across anything that makes you feel uncomfortable, tell a trusted adult. You might need to consider reporting the content if you feel that it violates any rules or policies.

- Remember the importance of not oversharing or giving out private information.

Online Gaming

The online gaming world is incredibly big and diverse. An activity that is available on a variety of devices and consoles, online gaming allows players to connect through the internet and converse with each other through headphones while playing. It is a huge industry which garners massive followings, hosts worldwide events and conventions, and produces millions of pounds worth of merchandising. It is particularly popular with – but not limited to – young boys.

Examples of popular consoles include:

- Xbox
- Nintendo
- PlayStation
- Desktop computers (PCs)

Examples of popular games include:

- World of Warcraft (roleplaying)
- Minecraft
- Halo
- Destiny
- Grand Theft Auto
- Fortnite

DID YOU KNOW?

It is estimated that 5% of young people in The Netherlands are addicted to online gaming.[7]

Research at the University of Amsterdam used the following nine criteria[8] (taken from the internet gaming disorder scale from the Diagnostic and Statistical Manual of Mental Disorders (DSM-5)) to assess whether young people were addicted:

- Preoccupation: spending substantial amounts of time thinking about gaming.

- Tolerance: needing to spend an increasing amount of time to feel the desired effect (excitement, etc.).

- Withdrawal: feeling restless, irritated, angry, frustrated, anxious or sad when unable play games.

- Persistence: unsuccessful attempts to stop, control or reduce the amount of the time spent gaming.

- Escape: using gaming to relieve negative moods.
- Problems: ongoing usage despite being aware of negative consequences.
- Deception: lying or covering up the extent of usage.
- Displacement: reduced social or recreational activities as a result of continued gaming.
- Conflict: losing or nearly losing an important relationship or opportunity.

In this study, the average teenager was found to spend three hours on social media platforms and another three hours playing computer games per day. The Netherlands was the first European country to get broadband internet, so it is likely that other countries will follow suit with these trends. And that's worrying!

CONCERNS

Online gaming comes with some real worries for parents and carers, including:

- Addiction to gaming.
- Desensitisation, especially to violent or misogynistic content
- Isolation and reduced amount of time socialising in the real world.
- Lack of physical exercise and movement.
- A decline in educational performance or slipping of grades.
- Underage children accessing age-restricted games.
- Children talking to strangers online who might potentially exploit them.

- Spending money on credits / features to use in games.
- Impact on sleep – not only are screens and exciting games over-stimulating, making going to sleep difficult, there is always someone to play with in a global community across different time zones.

TIPS FOR MANAGING YOUR USE OF ONLINE GAMES:

- Restrict gaming time to certain hours of the day, and for a certain number of hours per day or week.
- Make the active decision to have leisure time offline and try to socialise with friends face-to-face.
- Make sure that you are not playing any games for which you are underage.

CHAPTER 2

THE POSITIVES OF SOCIAL MEDIA

The internet is a place full of creativity, energy and endless possibility! There is so much information out of there, and it can help people find support systems when they need it most. The internet can be a fantastic tool that allows you to stay in touch with friends, express ourselves, learn new things and share the things we love!

This book isn't about making social media look scary or telling you not to use it. In fact, it's very important for you to understand the positive things about the internet too, so that you and your family can make the most of it if you do choose to make social media a part of your day-to-day life.

If you're reading this book, the chances are that either you or the adults in your life are concerned about how you can make the most out of the internet and social media. There may be concerns in your family about this which might make it difficult to consider the positives. How can you make sure that you make the most out of the internet?

This chapter in no way covers all the wonderful possibilities and opportunities that the online world provides, but below are a just a few ways in which you can benefit from digital technology.

1. For some people, social media can be good for mental health! Yes, really! It has been known to:

- Decrease loneliness and depression and enhance self-esteem and confidence, through connecting with others and feeling part of a community.

- Help young people experiment with self-identity and self-expression in a safe and positive way. Perhaps you feel a bit too worried or nervous to tell your friends or family something about yourself right now. Maybe you're confused about who and what you might be as a person, and you want to figure it out. The internet can help you experiment with expressing yourself, but you need to be careful and thoughtful about how and where you do this.

- Help people feel supported and part of a wider group or network.

- Provide opportunities for young people with mental health difficulties to discuss their symptoms and experiences online. This can you help you to feel less alone, get some advice where it's safe and appropriate to do so, and alleviate some of the isolation and anxiety that comes with suffering with mental health issues alone. Again, you need to find safe and helpful places to do this.

2. The internet can help you build an extra social network:

- You might find that you're more comfortable talking online than face-to-face, especially if you're shy or you struggle with social anxiety.

- It might give you a way to stay connected to others, even during times that are difficult.

- It can help you stay in touch with friends or family who might live a long distance away from you.

3. You can find helpful and useful information online:

- Social media can provide you with information about the wider world that you might never have otherwise known. It's a great way to learn about other ways of life, different countries, and new interests and activities.

- It gives you quick access to support lines, advice pages and chat forums hosted by charities and other organisations designed to support young people. This is particularly helpful if you need help with your mental health, your social life, worries with schoolwork or questions about your future career.

4. The internet can be a great source of knowledge, and it can help you with your education and gain more skills:

- It can provide access to educational apps and websites, which are great for revision and further learning.

- It can spark the imagination and help you enjoy learning in different ways.

- The internet can give you control over how you access and remember information. You can use it to find websites that fit with your learning style. Some people like to read information, whereas others like to watch videos or hear spoken information.

- As long as apps and websites are an add-on to – and not instead of – face-to-face interaction and learning, there's no reason you can't use them to help you with your homework. Just make sure you use educational apps (and even games!) in moderation, and make sure it doesn't distract you from your homework.

- You can use the internet to discover what jobs you might want to pursue in the future, and find out what character traits and skills you would need.

5. The internet can spark creativity both online and offline:

- You can find lots of new ideas about what activities and hobbies to take part in and enjoy in your spare time. Want to find out local places to visit, a new kind of craft to try, or a new sport to take part in? Do you want to find local classes where you can make new friends? The internet is a great place for finding information on this!

- Platforms such as YouTube and other websites can help you discover, develop and nurture new practical skills. You can find written and video tutorials online.

- Websites, forums, blogs, vlogging sites and video streaming apps provide a platform for you to create and share content. What a great way to find your own identity and develop your own unique voice!

DID YOU KNOW?

The internet can help you get involved with political or social causes and movements that mean a lot to you.

30% of 12 to 15-year-olds who use the internet have signed petitions or shared / talked about the news on social media and engaged in civic participation[9].

Some social media can be incredibly inspiring for young people. There are a whole host of teenagers who have used the power of social media for good, such as challenging global companies, promoting equality, raising awareness, and making change at a staggering level!

CHAPTER 3

THE DARKER SIDE OF THE INTERNET

It's likely that the adults in your life have some worries about your use of the internet. The sad truth is that there are risks when you are online. Your job is to be able to show the adults in your life that you understand these risks and are able to keep yourself safe, just like when you are out and about in the real world. Would you have a conversation with a dodgy looking adult that you have never met before, or would you wonder why they are talking to you and what they might be thinking, and move away? Your parents, carers or teachers will probably be less stressed if they know you understand their concerns and how to manage them. They also want to feel reassured that if anything does go wrong, you can talk to them so that they can help you or anyone else who might need support.

Listed below are some of the negative or more dangerous things that you could find online. You may have come across them already. There are also some tips and pointers about what to do if you find yourself dealing with any of the more unpleasant things out there on the internet.

CYBERBULLYING (OR ONLINE BULLYING)

We all know what bullying is, whether we have or we haven't encountered it ourselves. Cyberbullying (or online bullying) is the same as any other form of bullying. The difference here is that it happens online or via a mobile phone instead. Bullies can make themselves anonymous online, so sometimes people feel free to write things that they wouldn't say face-to-face. This can lead to some very hurtful and nasty comments, and they can be very isolating. Left undealt with, it can start to have a really negative effect on your emotional wellbeing or your mental health.

Why is cyberbullying so dangerous?

Whereas in the real world, where people can physically escape or hide from bullying outside of school, college or at home, it is a lot more difficult to step away from cyberbullying. The virtual world can be accessed anytime, anywhere, and often you'll find that no matter how hard you try, you can't quite get away from it.

What can really make it worse is that bullies can set up anonymous or fake profiles so that people can't track down their true identity. And because there's no teacher, parent or any other kind of authority that you can always see online, often people will send messages or do horrible things without a second thought about the consequences.

The fact that people can't see the immediate effects of cyberbullying right in front of them also often means that people will take bullying a lot further online than they would in real life.

When online, cyberbullies often feel less of a responsibility to behave in the right way. Some young people say that the internet is the one area of their lives that they do not feel has clear expectations or standards of behaviour that they should stick to.[10]

It can be difficult for social media platforms to monitor what people are saying to each other, so sometimes the bullying can remain for everyone to see for long periods of time. It can also appear across many websites with a wide audience. This can make it feel more humiliating.

DID YOU KNOW?

Cyberbullying is one of the biggest challenges to young people online, with one study showing that 17% of 12 to 20-year-olds in the UK in 2017 had reported experiencing cyberbullying, based on their own definition.[11]

Some online messaging apps can be worse than others for inviting cyberbullying, especially those that allow you to make anonymous accounts. There are lots of people out there campaigning for Google and Apple to take some of them, such as Sarahah and Sayat, off their platforms.[12] But there are new ones being built all the time, so it's up to you to stay vigilant and it's up to your parent(s) or guardian(s) to help you.

If left undealt with, cyberbullying can lead to mental health difficulties. Some people even delete their social media profile or stop using it because of cyberbullying.[13] At its worst it has led young people to feel depressed and anxious, and it has even caused suicide. It is dangerous.

REMEMBER:

Cyberbullying doesn't have to be a normal part of growing up.

Managing Cyberbullying

In a similar way to "playground" bullying, cyberbullying is often very difficult to control, though there are organisations and schemes which are tackling the issue in countries all over the world. One example is the Stop, Speak, Support campaign in the UK – launched in 2017 by Prince William, the Duke of Cambridge – which talks about what to do "when the banter turns bad".[14]

It recommends that people should "Stop" (do not share or like negative comments and check the community guidelines), "Speak" (talk to a trusted adult, use the report button on the site, and / or talk to a children's helpline) and "Support" – send a supportive message to the person being bullied, spend some time with them, and encourage them to talk with an adult.

But perhaps you're unsure whether or not you or someone else is being cyberbullied? Or maybe you just want to know what to look out for so that, if it happens to you or someone you know, you can nip it in the bud early on? Here are some examples of cyberbullying behaviour:

- Posting a nasty comment on a profile / photo
- Sending a horrible or abusive private message
- Bullying people on an online game
- Humiliation
- Wrongfully reporting profiles
- Spreading rumours about people online
- Sharing someone's personal information against their will

- Sharing photos or videos of people that they don't like
- Cropping people out of photos or not including someone in a chat
- Pressuring someone into doing something they don't want to do, such as posting sexually explicit photos
- Impersonating someone else online to get them in trouble or ruin their reputation
- "Fraping" or hacking someone else's account in order to do them harm
- Creating malicious websites about a person in order to target them

What do I do if I'm being cyberbullied?

- Don't respond.
- Talk to a trusted adult. They can – and will – help you. You will not get in trouble for being cyberbullied.
- If you feel there is no one in your life you can talk to, you can look up local bullying support charities, such as Childline.
- Take a screenshot of the bullying and keep a record of it.
- Report them to social media platform – get a trusted adult to help you if you're unsure how to do this.
- If you receive bullying emails, these can be reported to your email account provider – check the account details for an email address to report it to. An adult can help you with this.
- If you receive text messages, keep them so they can be used as examples of what you are experiencing.
- Don't shut down your account. If things are becoming distressing and overwhelming, suspend it if possible until you've dealt with it.

I'm cyberbullying someone and I feel bad about it. What should I do?

- Delete any nasty posts, statuses, tweets, comments, or messages where possible. See if you can post something genuinely positive instead.

- Apologise. It's a brave thing to do, but you'll really help the victim feel better and more supported.

- Encourage others to stop, if you're able to.

- Try not to beat yourself up about it – see it as an opportunity to learn. The important thing is that you recognise that what you've done is harmful and you've taken steps to try to repair this.

- Think about what made you do it. Are you struggling with something yourself? Do you feel bad about yourself? Has someone bullied you? How can you help yourself to feel more positive?

- Seek advice from a trusted adult if you're unsure or nervous. They will appreciate your honesty and be proud that you're willing to learn from your mistakes.

REMEMBER:

Be nice to others! Sending negative comments to others has a huge impact; think about this before you post. You are also more likely to be on the receiving end of negative comments if you're nasty to others. Help make the internet be a supportive place for everyone to be.

There are often clear signs that someone you know is being cyberbullied. Here are some to look out for:

- A big change in their behaviour

- A change in the amount of time they spend on social media or computers

- Appearing more upset or angry than is normal, especially after using the internet or their phone
- An unwillingness to go to school
- Secrecy about their online activity and / or avoidance of talking about social media[15]
- Eating or sleeping less

I'm worried that my friend is being cyberbullied. How can I tell someone and how can I help?

Offer support to people you see being bullied – send them a nice message, ask them if they'd like to talk about their experience, and check that they have asked an adult for help. If they feel unable to talk with an adult perhaps they can get support from Childline (www.childline.org.uk) or an equivalent in your country. It's also worth encouraging them to step away from their phone or device for a little while and spend some quality time with you, face-to-face.

FOMO (FEAR OF MISSING OUT)

This is a growing phenomenon among young people, and it's likely that you or someone you know have experienced this. FOMO (fear of missing out) is that feeling that a person gets when they're worried that other people are enjoying fun events or gatherings when you aren't or can't be there to enjoy it too. It is often triggered by posts on social media. This can sometimes cause people to feel like they might be "missing out" on life. It can cause anxiety and feelings of inadequacy.

It has also been linked to internet addiction. In an attempt to avoid feeling FOMO, some people spend longer and longer periods of time online – sometimes well into the night – in order to feel as though they're not missing out on anything.

It's important to remember, though, that a lot of what people post online isn't always the absolute truth.

They are capturing a point in time, most likely a moment that was short lived and / or artificial.

GROOMING AND ONLINE CHILD SEXUAL EXPLOITATION

It is a sad and unfortunate reality that sexual abuse and grooming happens online, and it is a very real risk all over the world. By making yourself aware of these dangers, you can help keep yourself safe.

What is grooming and online child sexual exploitation?

Online "grooming" is when someone makes an emotional connection a person in order to misuse that trust. Groomers will often be really nice and kind, complimenting someone, showing them support, and / or offering them things to gain their trust. A groomer might also encourage a person to fall out or lose trust in their friends and family, so that the groomer is the only person they can turn to. Then they are able to manipulate someone into doing things that oversteps boundaries.

A groomer can be someone you know or someone you don't. They can easily hide their real identity and pretend to be the same age as you, so that some of their requests sound completely normal.

If you're not aware of grooming or unsure of the signs to look out for, that can make you vulnerable, because it's often quite hard to spot. And groomers can gather lots of information about you if you share your personal information on your profiles. Sometimes they might request to meet you in person. They might seek out signs of insecurity, low self-esteem or neediness[16].

As outlined by the NSPCC, online child sexual exploitation involves a young person being persuaded to:

- Post sexually explicit images of themselves
- Take part in sexual activities using a camera (webcam, mobile phone), or
- Have sexual conversations online[17].
- Don't shut down your account. If things are becoming distressing and overwhelming, suspend it if possible until you've dealt with it.

Once an abuser has an image of you, they can then use it to force you into doing more and more dangerous things. They will often make threats if you refuse to do something they want, like threatening to send an image of you to your friends or family, or saying they will hurt people you know if you tell anyone. It can then become very difficult to feel able to ask for help from a trusted adult.

How can I reduce the chance of being groomed?

It can happen to anyone, and groomers can be very sophisticated. You might not even be aware it is taking place. But you can do the following:

- Look out for the signs as outlined above.

- Keep your personal information private and put privacy settings into place. Get a trusted adult to help you if you're unsure how to do this.

- Treat strangers online as you would do in real life. Be wary. Do not share personal information with people you do not know.

- Remember that just because someone is being nice to you, that doesn't mean they're trustworthy.

- Trust your instincts – if something doesn't feel right then end the chat.

- Never share sensitive information or sexually explicit photos or content with anyone, especially if you don't know them in real life.

- Be aware that if you post negative things about your life online (e.g. arguments with your family, saying you hate members of your family) you may appear vulnerable and be targeted. Think carefully before you share.

DID YOU KNOW?

- In 2016, 5% of 12 to 15-year-olds in the UK had sent a picture or video of themselves to someone they had only met online.

- 4% had sent personal information (such as name and address)[18].

Although this could be entirely innocent, it might make you a target. Often people don't realise the risk they are taking.

What should I do if I'm being groomed or abused?

- Tell a trusted adult as soon as possible.

- Keep in mind that you will not get in trouble for anything that's happened / is happening.

- No matter what threats have been made or how unsafe you feel there is always a way out, and trusted adults can help you.

- Keep records of it – don't delete any accounts or posts.

- Use support organisations such as Childline or NSPCC, or the equivalent in your country, who will give you advice or help you file a report.

EXPOSURE TO DISTURBING, INAPPROPRIATE OR TRAUMATISING CONTENT

The internet is a huge and varied place, and there's a very real possibility that you might accidentally come across unpleasant content, such as violence, pornography, sexually explicit material, and websites promoting things like self-harm and eating disorders. You don't have to search too far to find pictures and videos of people being hurt, depictions of self-harm or websites promoting eating disorders. It's so easy to accidentally click onto something you didn't mean to see, or you might go looking for these things.

This kind of content is not only upsetting, but it can affect your mood and your mental health. The key is knowing what habits you can pick up that help you avoid coming across some of this content.

How do I avoid seeing disturbing or inappropriate content online?

- Use filters. On some apps, such as Twitter, you can opt not to see certain words, images, or offensive content on your feeds. Check your social media app's FAQ's or privacy settings and look for the filter options.

- Block pop-ups on your app or internet browser. There are many different ways to do this; get an adult to help you out if you're unsure.

- Avoid click-bait (an enticing headline often used on dodgy sites that make you really want to click on the link).

- Don't take the risk. If you're unsure of a site, or if someone sends you link or recommends a site that you think might have violent or inappropriate material on it, don't click it – even if they encourage you to do so.

- Think carefully – once you've seen something disturbing you can never change that. You are in charge of whether you see it or not, even if others are encouraging you.

I accidentally came across some upsetting content, and now I can't get it out of my head. What can I do?

- You might find that the image keeps popping into your mind when you don't want or expect it to. Try to talk with someone you trust about what you saw as this will help. If the image upsets you, just acknowledge the emotion and let it pass without trying to avoid it or stop the feeling. It's likely that in time the image will stop coming into your mind.

- It might help you to ask an adult to support you to report the content so that it can be removed.

- Take a break from the internet and reconnect with the real world – do something physical (go for a walk, play a sport, paint, bake).

"SEXTING" AND REVENGE PORN

"Revenge porn" is the term used to describe when someone takes photos or videos of a sexual nature and shares them online without that person's agreement. In 2015, the UK brought in a law that made "revenge porn" illegal.

With the rise of "sexting", it's important that you understand the risks and potential consequences of sending such private material to others, even if it's your boyfriend, girlfriend, or someone else you trust. Remember, relationships change and even if you trust them when you share images this may not always be the case. Once you send an image you have lost control of it.

Revenge porn sometimes happens when a couple splits up or as a result of online or cyberbullying. Sometimes you can get the material taken down, but quite often it's been seen by lots of people before then.

Facebook and Instagram have a zero tolerance policy and will report anyone posting sexually explicit images if it is believed a child is involved.

Children as young as 11 years old have been victims of revenge porn.

DID YOU KNOW?
30% of 15-year-olds have sent a naked photo of themselves at least once[19].

What if I become the victim of revenge porn?

- Tell a trusted adult straight away, even if it feels difficult and you are worried about how they might react. The quicker you let them know, the quicker the situation can be managed. It will be easier if you tell them first rather than them coming across it or someone else telling them.

- Keep screenshots as evidence.

- Report it to the website or app if possible.

- As revenge porn is very serious and now illegal in the UK, some European countries and in a number of US states, you may also choose to report it to the police, so make sure you keep screenshots and records of any incidents.

- Update your social media privacy settings, so that your content is safer and cannot be misused again.

- If you feel you need to, block anyone who is harassing you as a result.

- If appropriate, seek help from dedicated support lines such as www.revengepornhelpline.org.uk in the UK, or www.cybercivilrights.org in the US, who can help you figure out the best course of action.

NEGATIVE IMPACT ON CHILDREN'S MENTAL HEALTH

DID YOU KNOW?

Royal Society for Public Health developed a league table for the impact of social media platforms on mental health, based on 14 factors. These factors included whether the platforms made a positive or negative contribution to things such as sleep, anxiety, depression, self expression and identity, loneliness, fear of missing out, bullying and real-world relationships.

Overall, YouTube was found to have the most positive impact. This was followed by Twitter, Facebook, Snapchat and Instagram – all of which had an overall negative impact, especially on sleep.

Young people aged
14-24
reported that
Youtube was the most positive social media app for health and wellbeing
(Royal Society for Public Health, 2017)

It probably comes as no surprise that the internet can negatively affect your mental health, especially if you're unaware of the dangers or how to avoid them. Social media changes so rapidly and it's important to think about how it might affect your wellbeing.

Young people now are sharing more about themselves online than they typically would offline. You may be putting yourself out there more on social media, which means you have a much wider audience than if you did so offline. This means there are more people who might make negative comments or be unpleasant. People online are much more likely to be forward or aggressive, particularly when they are anonymous, compared to face-to-face (known as the online disinhibition effect[20]). You need to think carefully about what and where you chose to post and how you might feel if you do get negative (or perhaps even no) feedback. If you wouldn't share something with friends offline, should you share it online in an open forum?

Depression and anxiety

Research seems to be mixed, but some has shown that negative feedback on friend networking sites can decrease self-esteem and wellbeing.[21] The possible harmful effects of social networking on adolescents include increased exposure to harm, social isolation and depression.[22] But, other research has found no association between social networking site use and depression in older adolescents[23] (American university students). A review of the relationship between social networking and depression found that it was complicated, and it could be both positive and negative.

Another study of secondary school pupils in the UK found that those who used social media more often – and those who were more emotionally invested in social media – had poorer quality sleep, lower self-esteem and higher levels of anxiety and depression[24].

If you rely too much on social media to make you feel good and spend a lot of time on it, then it is likely to have a negative effect on you.

For young people who are socially anxious, the internet can provide a way to connect with others, which feels less threatening. It can feel easier to share online[25]. But it is difficult to present a genuine picture of yourself online when there are worries about how you will be seen. Those who present a fake self online are more likely to suffer from anxiety and poor social skills[26]. Whilst there is a place for connecting with others online it is really important for you to make offline, real relationships. This is even more important if you feel nervous in social situations so that you can develop your confidence.

As with everything it is a mixed picture and depends on lots of different things including the support you have and what sort of person you are. The internet can have benefits but it can also be negative for your mental health. Too much of anything can be bad, so notice when and why you use the internet and how it makes you feel before, during and after. We'll cover this more later.

Body image issues or having negative feelings about your body

Social media can have a real impact on confidence and body image. There are many heavily edited photos and videos online which enforce the idea that children and young people are unable to live up to other people's standards, leaving them feeling inadequate and self-conscious about their looks, skills or even personalities.

How often do you post something online when you are having a difficult day, and how often do you post the good moments? And how often do you look at other people's online lives and think about how good they look? The online world is giving a biased impression of real life, and it can cause you to compare yourself, unfairly, to other people. Often that's a really unpleasant feeling and it can leave you feeling awful about your own body or sense of identity.

It's fine to post the good things online, but it helps to remember that no one is perfect, and that often the content you're exposed to online is heavily edited.

Research has shown that Facebook photo activity is associated with body image disturbance in adolescent girls[27]. The amount of time spent posting and viewing photos was linked to thinking patterns about wanting to be thin and thinking about yourself as an object rather than a person. It was also linked to being less satisfied with your weight.

It is not the amount of time spent on Facebook but the amount of time dedicated to photo activity which predicts body dissatisfaction. It does not mean that this causes poor body image, but rather it may be an outward way of showing it.

Think about how much time you spend looking at images and how it makes you feel. If it makes you feel good then that's okay. If it makes you feel bad about yourself, then you need to stop and find some ways to make a positive relationship with your body instead. Focus on the parts of your body that you like. Find a sport or activity that you enjoy and makes you feel good. Go for a walk and appreciate all that your body can do. Limit your exposure to material that makes you feel inadequate.

If you feel very strongly negative about your body to the point that you feel it is affecting your day-to-day life or your mental health, tell a trusted adult who will be able to help you get the support you need.

DID YOU KNOW?

In 2017, Ditch the Label's survey found that 42% of young people thought it was always okay to edit a selfie before posting it online – and therefore present a false image to the online community.[28]

ADDICTION TO THE INTERNET AND SOCIAL MEDIA

Social media can be fun. It's a great way to keep in contact with your friends, find new hobbies, and keep yourself entertained. But you probably wouldn't be surprised to learn that some experts say screens are like "digital heroin or cocaine" to children and young people! Of course, gaining followers, likes, and positive comments online feels good, but social media can become so addictive, in fact, that people can spend excessive amounts of time on it and struggle to pull themselves away.

Addiction to social media is serious, though, and it can be very damaging. It can have a knock-on effect in other areas of people's lives, such as performance at school, relationships, and physical and emotional health. The more hours you spend staring at screens, especially when sitting indoors, the less time you spend on studying, sleeping, going outside and getting some exercise, socialising in real life, doing some other kind of activity, and / or sleeping!

You may also find yourself being addicted to text messaging or messaging apps, finding it hard to cut down on it, losing sleep and lying about the amount of time you are spending on it. You might even find you are having neck pain, called "text neck"[29].

Addiction to online gaming is a problem too. Games are designed to keep you hooked (they release a neurotransmitter called dopamine which makes you feel good, and the hormone adrenaline which gives you a rush) and if you are playing online with others this might make it even harder to stop. At its most extreme, online gaming addiction can lead to psychiatric disorders where there is a blurring between reality and fantasy[30]. Gaming can impact sleep and take up time that needs to be spent doing other things like homework. Be very careful about how much time you are spending on gaming and whether it is stopping you from doing things in other parts of your life. If you find it hard to stop and it's causing conflict in your family, then it's time to rethink how you use it.

In the "How to Manage Your Internet Use" section of this book, we will talk in more detail about how you can better manage the amount of time you spend on social media and the internet, so that you can use it in a healthy and productive way.

DID YOU KNOW?

One out of every two teens in a 2016 US survey felt addicted to his or her device, and the majority of parents within the study (59%) felt that their kids were addicted.[31]

Research has also shown that the mere presence of a mobile phone reduces concentration[32], so you don't even have to be actively using it for it to have an impact.

CHAPTER 4

HOW TO MANAGE YOUR INTERNET USE

The internet can be an amazing and inspiring place where you can connect with people all over the world. But there can also be a negative side to it, with young people becoming addicted and falling victim to cyber bullying and online abuse. The internet was never developed with young people in mind, so you need to make sure that you can use the internet and social media in a safe way. Your brain is also going through a huge period of change and you need to look after it – too much screen time may have a long-lasting effect on this.

We would like you to be:

Internet savvy: Understand the risks involved in using the internet and be aware of how you can protect yourself and others.

Digitally resilient: Be able to recognise and manage when negative things happen online.

Responsible users: Use the internet for good and be able to enjoy the benefits of it knowing that you are creating a digital footprint that will last into the future.

HOW, WHEN, WHY AND WHERE

It might be useful to first think about how, when, why and where you are using the internet and social media. How is that working out for you? Do you think you have a good balance in your life, both online and offline?

Perhaps you're worried that your use of social media is having a negative impact on you. Do you feel like you might be addicted to the internet? Would you like to use it in a more positive way? Do you feel unsafe when you're on your phone or device? Perhaps you want to try other things but find you don't have time? Maybe you're worried that if you don't stay online as much as possible, you'll get left behind or left out of your friendship group?

First, you might want to use the space in this book, or use a separate piece of paper, to take some time and answer the following questions honestly:

- **How do you use the internet and social media?**

_____

_____

- **Are you mostly using a mobile phone, tablet or PC?**

_____

_____

_____

- **Which websites and apps do you prefer to use?**

_____

_____

_____

_____

- **Why do you prefer to use these?**

_____

_____

_____

_____

- **What are your family's rules for how you can use technology at home?**

_____

_____

_____

- **When do you use it?**

_____

_____

_____

- **How often do your use your device(s)?**

_____

_____

- **When do you first check your social media in the morning?**

_____

_____

_____

- **When is the last time you check it at night?**

_____

_____

- **Do you find it hard to go to sleep?**

  _____

- **Do you keep devices with you when you sleep? Do you check them at night?**

  _____

  _____

- **How long can you go for without checking your phone / tablet?**

  _____

  _____

- **Do you feel an urge to check social media often? What happens if you resist it?**

  _____

  _____

  _____

- **Why do you use it?**

  _____

- **Why do you use the internet and social media?**

  _____

  _____

- **How do you think it makes your life better?**

_____

- **What do you think your life would be like if you used it less?**

_____

_____

- **Do you have FOMO?**

_____

- **Do you live through your phone, or can you be in the moment?**

_____

_____

- **Are you online because it feels better than life offline? If so, why does it feel better than offline?**

_____

_____

- **Do you ever retreat into the virtual world because the real world isn't that great?**

_____

_____

Now, think about what you would like to change. For each of the answers to these questions, write down what you would ideally like to do, even it that doesn't differ from your current answers. That will help you think about what steps you need to take next and which of the following practical tips you'd like to act upon.

_____

_____

_____

_____

_____

_____

_____

_____

_____

_____

_____

_____

_____

_____

_____

_____

_____

_____

_____

_____

_____

_____

_____

_____

_____

_____

_____

_____

_____

_____

_____

_____

TAKING STEPS TO IMPROVE YOUR USE OF SOCIAL MEDIA AND THE INTERNET

Below are some tips that might help you navigate the digital world in a way that makes you feel happier and safer. It's up to you which you choose to adopt and which you don't.

Try having an honest discussion with your parent / carer about your internet use and how they see it.

1. **Take active steps to make time for activities and hobbies that don't require you to be online.**

This will help you keep up your concentration levels and will stop you from feeling bored by the real world or whenever you're not switched on. You could take this time to read books, do some crafting, playing a sport you love, going to see a film, or socialising face-to-face with friends.

2. **If your family sets up rules, curfews or a social media plan at home, stick to them.**

    This might feel difficult at times, but they are doing it for your wellbeing, and taking the time away from your device will be very good for your mental health. Ask your parent / carer about rules they disliked when they were younger, but they now they see as helpful for them!

3. **Turn off your phone, or put it away, at least two hours before bedtime.**

Research has shown that looking at a screen has a negative impact on sleep. The light from the screens on mobile phones, laptops, tablets etc. stops your body from producing melatonin (a hormone that helps you feel sleepy and is produced when it gets dark).

You can switch your device to night mode, which reduces the amount of blue light that emanates from your screen, but this won't stop the stimulation that you get from being online. Having a good sleep routine which doesn't involve devices is helpful, and sleep is important for everyone, but particularly for you as your body grows and changes take place in your brain.

4. **Make a rule that you will check your phone only after a certain amount of time after you wake up and before you go to sleep. Stick to it as much as possible.**

For example, you might decide that you will only check your phone after you've had your breakfast or showered in a morning. This not only helps you exercise your self-discipline, but helps prevent you from feeling like a slave to your device or social media.

5. **Turn your phone off (or, if it feels safer, put it away somewhere safe) during certain times of the day, and tell your friends or family when you'll be available.**

Perhaps you'd like to keep your phone off during lunch time or break time when you want to spend time with your friends, or some time during the evening when you want to wind down. This will help break your dependence, but allow you some head space, away from the constant pull and pressure of social media.

6. **Uninstall apps and / or avoid websites that make you feel bad.**

7. **Remind yourself that photos and videos are often heavily edited online to make people's lives look ideal.**

   Try to avoid comparing yourself to what you see on your feed.

8. **Keep in mind that you can't always go to every social event or be part of every conversation, and that that doesn't mean that you're not still part of your friendship group.**

   If you feel a sense of FOMO, then try creating opportunities for yourself to enjoy. Arrange something with friends or try a new activity.

9. **Address or seek out help for any real-world issues you might be facing online.**

   Perhaps you find social media, the internet or gaming very addictive and appealing because you're using it to hide or escape from things that you're finding difficult in the real world. Some distraction from this is okay in the form of internet use, but not if it is creating problems in other areas of your life. Avoidance works in the short term, but it usually creates more difficulties in the long term. Think about people who might be able to support you and help to confront these difficulties.

   For example, we've already seen how turning to the online world if you are socially anxious actually makes things worse. The most helpful thing to do is find ways to connect with others in the real world to build your confidence. Sometimes the reason why a problem starts is different to the reason the problem keeps going.

   So, you might turn to social media or online gaming because you feel lonely, but you may continue to use these platforms because you become addicted. Because you are addicted, you then have less time to meet new people and so you feel even more isolated. This downward spiral could then lead to mental health difficulties.

Thinking about why you are lonely in the first place (e.g. you find it difficult to meet new people, feel socially awkward, haven't found the right group of friends) will help you change things (develop your social skills by practising, watch how other people interact, take some risks and try out new activities to meet like minded people) and help make you less likely to rely on the internet.

If there are difficulties which you are facing that feel huge and you think that there isn't an adult in your life who you could turn to, you could speak with Childline www.childline.org.uk (or the equilivalent in your country) or see if your school / college has a counselling service.

Believe me, no matter how bad things feel, there is always someone who can help.

THINK ABOUT GOOD ONLINE CONDUCT

Here's a way to think about what you do online, and how to make sure you're managing yourself in a positive way.

STOP!

Step away from the device! Breathe!

THINK

Take a moment to consider:

- What are you hoping to achieve?
- What are the possible positives and negatives?
- What will it say about you now and in the future?
- What impact will it have on others?
- How will you manage if a post gets negative comments or no likes?
- Are you keeping yourself and others safe?

DO

What will you do now? Will you change your behaviour or go ahead, having considered the consequences? Make sure you are doing the right thing in the moment, and also for the long term.

Below are some tips to help you make some positive decisions.

How do I choose what content I should post on my profiles?

Think hard before posting anything online and consider the following questions. The answers will help you make a more thoughtful decision that you can take responsibility for:

- Think very carefully before posting or sending images of yourself to others. Are they images you'd be happy to lose control over?

- Think about what could happen to a sexually explicit or embarrassing photo. Imagine if you fell out with the person you sent it to and they decided to share it or threatened to do so. How would you feel if it was sent to your friends or family?

- Think about whether you might want a particular image available to others in one, five or even 10 years' time. What if an employer came across it in the future? Remember you create a digital footprint that can be hard to undo.

- Does your intended status or comment include private information? Could it potentially be used to harm you in some way, such as identity theft, security threats or grooming?

How can I make sure I'm not hurting anyone else?

It's always best to think twice before you post anything, especially when you're feeling angry or upset. It can be hard in the heat of the moment, but before posting a comment or message to someone, step away from your device for a short while and take a deep breath. Think:

- Will this hurt their feelings?
- Do I really mean this?
- Could this count as cyberbullying?
- What will the consequences be for me?
- Would I say this to the person in real life?

Now what will you do? After considering these questions, will you think ahead? If you have already posted something in the heat of the moment, will you change or delete your post or message? Will you apologise?

How can I feel safer online?

The best way to feel completely safe online is to stay resilient and be digitally savvy. Protect yourself as much as possible:

- Never give personal information about yourself or others to someone that you don't know.
- Alert the relevant people if you feel you're being cyberbullied, and keep out of conversations where you feel that cyberbullying is taking place.
- Make sure you have checked your privacy settings on your profiles so that only your friends can view your information, and think about what you are posting on public forums.
- Think carefully about friend requests and why someone might be asking to connect with you. Are they really your friends? Are they missing a profile photo? Look at their activity if you can – do they comment a lot on "sexy" or sexual photos? Do they post aggressive or mean statuses?
- Make sure your passwords are strong (a combination of characters, letters and symbols and not easy to guess) and don't give them to anyone – even your boyfriend, girlfriend, partner or best friends.

- Remember that there are people on the internet who may want to take advantage of you.

- Always talk to a trusted adult if something doesn't feel right for yourself or others.

How can I use the internet effectively for my studies and education?

- Think carefully about where the information has come from and whether you can trust it.

- Ask your teachers and / or parent or carer to point you in the right direction of good websites and apps to use.

- When you are studying, try turning your phone off or having it another room so that you are not tempted to look at it.

How can I stop myself worrying about what people think about me online?

We are social beings, and we all think about what others think about us. Some people are less concerned by what others might think, whereas others feel overwhelmed by it. The same is true online. The difficulty is that, when sitting behind a device, you don't get feedback from people about how they are seeing your posts. It's also easy for people to misinterpret a post or message because we are missing the cues we usually use, such as tone of voice, body language, or the way somebody says something.

It's worth remembering that our thoughts feel true, but it doesn't mean that they are the truth.

- Have a conversation with yourself and challenge your thoughts. If you become worried about what someone is thinking online, as yourself what this might be about. What does it mean to you? Are you worried about whether someone likes you? Do you feel lonely and that comments / likes are a way to make up for this?

- Take some time away from the internet to try to get a different perspective.

- Remind yourself of your positive qualities, the things people like about you and the reasons not to worry about others.

- Be reassured that during your teenage years you are likely to become more worried about what other people think, as you develop your identity and become more certain of what and who you like.

- Try to make sure you have people in your life who help you to feel good about yourself and who can safely share your doubts with.

How can I make sure I'm taking care of my mental health while online?

- Make sure you are not spending too much time online. If your parent / carer is nagging you about this, then you need to pay attention to it, no matter how irritating they are!

- If you are finding it hard to reduce your time online, or it is getting in the way of other things, then ask for support.

- Notice if being online is making it more difficult to be in the moment or concentrate on everyday life offline. Too much stimulation online can then make the world seem slow and boring, and it may be a sign that you need less time online.

- Try to stay balanced – the world online is not as it seems, and it is unhelpful to compare yourself to those online. Remember, most people post more positives than negatives, so you are not getting the full story. And many people edit their photos!

- Remember the basics are important for good mental health – eat and sleep well and get regular exercise.

- Seek out help and support if you find that you're feeling low, anxious, depressed, or even suicidal.

Talk to a trusted adult who will listen to you and be able to help you.

- You or your parent / carer can ask for a referral to your local child and adolescent mental health service (CAMHS) if you are concerned about your mental health.

CHAPTER 5

AM I INTERNET SAVVY

Am I internet savvy? Am I digitally resilient? Am I a responsible social media user?

These are good questions to ask yourself, but perhaps you don't know the answer just yet. You might feel confident that you know about everything you need to know about the online world, but there may be some things you haven't thought about.

Below are some examples of some things you might want to consider about your use of social media.

AM I INTERNET SAVVY AND DIGITALLY RESILIENT?

To be internet savvy is to understand the risks involved in using the internet and being aware of how you can protect yourself and others. To be resilient is to be able to manage when things get difficult. Are you unsure if this is you? It might be worth thinking about the questions below.

Do you know what to do if you feel unsafe or experience or witness something negative?

CONSIDER: Do you know who you can turn to when you feel unsafe online? Are you worried that you might get into trouble or judged if you're part of – or witness something – negative online?

ACTION: Identify who you can talk to. It might be a family member or friend or someone at school or college. If it feels too hard to speak with someone in your support network, you can contact a helpline (for example, Childline or the equivalent in your country).

If someone dares you to do a potentially dangerous challenge online – for example, eating Tide Pods (washing tablets) or taking part in the Kylie Jenner Lip Challenge – do you feel confident enough to say no? Does peer pressure get the better of you?

CONSIDER: Why do you think it would be a good thing to do? Are there any benefits? Who do you want to impress by doing this? What are the potential risks or dangers? What if it goes wrong? What are the short and long term effects?

ACTION: Take some time to really think about your decision so that you can take responsibility for it. Is a prank that might gain some likes, or amuse some people for a moment, worth risking your health? Do some research so that you fully understand the risks, because the people you are trying to impress won't be affected – but you will.

What would you do if someone pressured you to send a picture?

CONSIDER: Do you feel confident enough, without fearing rejection, to say no when someone's pushing you for a photo you're uncomfortable sharing? Are you considering doing something because you want to or because you are worried about what will happen if you don't do it? Are you aware of the potential risks of exploitation or "revenge porn" that come with sexting?

ACTION: Bear in mind that there are risks that come with sexting. Remember that it is illegal for children under the age of consent (usually aged 16, but this can differ from country to country, so check the law where you live) to share sexually explicit photos.

Try to remember that you are in charge of your body, and you do not have to send a photo or video to anyone. If you're feeling pressured or unsafe, talk to an adult you trust. It is safer not to send an image, but if you do decide to go against advice and go ahead, then it is better not to include your face or any other identifiable features (for example tattoos, birth marks, personal objects in the background). Look at www.thinkuknow.co.uk for further advice.

27% of **12** to **15**-year-olds in the **UK** said that if they googled a website they would **trust it.** (Ofcom, 2017)

Maintain your curiosity – how do you know where the information comes from and how can you know if it is true?

CONSIDER: Are you aware that something isn't necessarily true just because it's online? Do you trust information, news or rumours just because they're being circulated on big or popular apps?

ACTION: Remember to always question things and be curious, especially if you plan on sharing or forwarding a post. Check the source and look for evidence for what you're reading or seeing. Can you look for safe and reliable sources to look it up before you share things?

Which sites do you like to go to, what games do you like to play, and which apps do you like to use?

CONSIDER: There might be a risk of you accidentally seeing traumatising, disturbing, or age-inappropriate content on any of these platforms. You might also come into contact with potentially dangerous individuals.

ACTION: Research or google any apps that you might feel unsure of, and explain to your parent, carer or teacher why you're concerned if anything worries you. They can advise you what signs to look out for and help you figure out if the app has any filters you can apply.

Do you edit your photos and if so, why?

CONSIDER: Why do you feel the need to edit your photos? Does seeing other people's polished selfies or perfect holiday pictures make you feel less attractive or inadequate? Think about what the person's intention was when they posted it – was it designed to make other people feel jealous? What are the parts of their life like that they don't share?

ACTION: Remember that a lot of photos and selfies online are Photoshopped, airbrushed, edited or tweaked to look better than in real life. Most people are very selective in what they share and the pictures do not reflect their entire life, but rather just a moment in time.

What does it mean to you get likes or comments on social media?

CONSIDER: How does it affect your self-confidence and mental wellbeing when you receive negative comments? How much of your self-worth or self-esteem is tied into likes and positive comments? How much time do you spend looking at images online?

ACTION: Think about how you balance the online and offline areas of your life. If you are relying too much on social media for your self-worth, it is a sign that you need to do more offline.

How do you show kindness and how do you avoid being unpleasant? Do you think it is okay to put negative comments online?

CONSIDER: Do you feel able to shake off an inevitable negative comment? Do you get very upset or affected by them? How do you respond to these sort of comments?

ACTION: Find ways to develop your confidence so that negative comments have less of an impact. Do things that make you feel good about yourself and that you feel a sense of achievement and pleasure in. Find out what these things are. Spend more time offline! Think about what you are posting and what your intention was – and it might give you more clues about why the negative comments are impacting you so much.

Ask yourself if you should always respond to negative comments and think about whether you are prepared to take the risk to receive negative comments by posting. Do you need to reconsider the material you are sharing?

What are you hoping to achieve when you post something?

CONSIDER: Perhaps something is going on for you that you're too scared to tell your parent or carer. Maybe you've done something you're not proud of. Maybe you have a big problem and you don't know who to speak to.

ACTION: If there is a trusted adult you feel comfortable talking to, let them know if you have any worries or problems. Tell them your worries about sharing – is it that you think you'll be punished or judged? Do you think you will risk damaging a relationship or end up feeling ashamed or humiliated? If it feels too difficult to talk to someone you know, you could seek out a school or college counsellor or contact a helpline.

AM I A RESPONSIBLE USER?

Do you know who to go and talk to if anything worries you?

CONSIDER: Do you understand the consequences of your actions if you put negative things online or are unpleasant to other social media users? Do you make positive and supportive comments?

ACTION: Remember that even though you're behind a screen, you are still talking to real people, and your words and actions will still have an impact. Would you say it to someone's face?

Do you know who to go and talk to if anything worries you?

CONSIDER: Is it important for you to get as many "likes" or equivalent as possible? Why do you need this form of validation? Do you want to be hurtful to someone? Are you doing something to please someone else, even if it makes you feel uncomfortable

ACTION: Think about your reasons for posting a particular status, photo, comment or message. Are any of them negative? Can you make it positive? How else can you express how you're feeling – or achieve self-confidence – without using social media first?

Are you being yourself online?

CONSIDER: Perhaps you're pretending to be very different than you actually are – or even another person altogether – while you're using the internet, gaming, or on social media. If you are doing this, why do you think that is? Do you feel inadequate, or are you doing something dangerous or unpleasant?

ACTION: It's okay to experiment with your identity, and we all behave slightly differently in different settings, but you need to make sure you are doing this in a safe way. Consider what kind of person you would like to be, which qualities are important to you, and how you can be true to them.

CHAPTER 6

HAVE A CONVERSATION

It's always useful to have a conversation with your parent, carer or teacher about social media and the internet, especially when you get your first mobile phone, tablet or computer. Talking can be beneficial for everyone, even if you feel fine managing yourself online. It's also a good idea to make sure you continue to talk to each other as time goes by, because some things can change very quickly and you might suddenly find yourself needing some support.

Of course you want to be to be digitally resilient, and you also want to feel safe when you go online. But sometimes you might be unsure of how to stay safe in different situations, especially if you come across some difficulties that you've never encountered before.

Very often your parent, carer or teacher will want to broach these subjects and ask you questions, so that they can also feel confident that they're supporting your use of the internet in any way that they can.

Maybe you just want to use this opportunity to reassure them that you will be safe and sensible, and that you know you can go to them if you ever feel differently. In my work with families, I usually find that the more willing a young person is to show that they understand risks and can identify ways to manage them, the more reassured adults feel and the more likely they are to give the young person some responsibility. Helping your parent / carer to feel that you are digitally savvy will hopefully mean there is more trust about your use of the internet. It will most likely work in your favour if you can show that you can be responsible online.

**If you found this book interesting ...
why not read this next?**

Social Media and Mental Health

Handbook for Parents and Teachers :)

Social Media and Mental Health Handbook for Parents and Teachers :) is the perfect resource for carers of teens on how to guide them through internet safety.

**If you found this book interesting ...
why not read this next?**

You can get our Social Media and Mental Health Handbooks as a two-book bundle.

Our Social Media and Mental Health Handbooks are invaluable in helping teenagers and their parents and carers to stay safe online.

REFERENCES

1 **Palfrey and Glasser.** (2008). *Born Digital: Understanding the First Generation of Digital Natives.* New York: Basic Books.

2 **Taspscott, D.** (2009). *Grown Up Digital.* London: McGraw Hill

3 **Ofcom.** (2016). *Children and Parents: Media Use and Attitudes Report.*

4 **Ofcom.** (2016). *Children and Parents: Media Use and Attitudes Report.*

5 www.bbc.co.uk/news/business-40424769, accessed 3rd July 2017

6 **Children's Commissioner.** *Growing Up Digital: A Report of the Growing Up Digital Taskforce.* London, 2017

7 **Jenner, F.** (2018). At least 5 % of young people suffer symptoms of social media addiction. [online] Horizon: the EU Research & Innovation magazine. Available at: https://horizon-magazine.eu/article/least-5-young-people-suffer-symptoms-social-media-addiction_en.html, accessed 1st Febuary 2018

8 **Jenner, F.** (2018). At least 5 % of young people suffer symptoms of social media addiction. [online] Horizon: the EU Research & Innovation magazine. Available at: https://horizon-magazine.eu/article/least-5-young-people-suffer-symptoms-social-media-addiction_en.html, accessed 1st Febuary 2018

9   **Livingstone, S.** (2018). The GDPR: Using evidence to unpack the implications for children online. [online] Media Policy Project. Available at: http://blogs.lse ac.uk/mediapolicyproject/2016/12/12/the-gdpr-using-evidence-to-unpack-the-implications-for-children-online/

10 www.stopspeaksupport.com/about/ accessed 25th January 2018

11 www.ditchthelabel.org/research-papers/the-annual-bullying-survey-2017/ accessed 24th January 2018

12 www.change.org/p/app-store-google-play-ban-apps-like-sarahah-where-my-daughter-was-told-to-kill-herself

13 www.ditchthelabel.org/research-papers/the-annual-bullying-survey-2017/ accessed 24th January, 2018

15 www.stopspeaksupport.com/about/ accessed 25th January, 2018

15 www.getcybersafe.gc.ca/cnt/cbrbllng/prnts/chld-bng-cbrblld-en.aspx

16 **Georgia M. Winters & Elizabeth L. Jeglic** (2017) Stages of Sexual Grooming: Recognizing Potentially Predatory Behaviors of Child Molesters, *Deviant Behavior*, 38:6, 724-733, DOI:10.1080/01639625.2016.1197656

17 www.nspcc.org.uk accessed 27th January, 2018

18 **Ofcom.** (2016). *Children and Parents: Media Use and Attitudes Report*

19 www.ditchthelabel.org/research-papers/the-wireless-report/

20 **Suler, J.** (2004). The online disinhibition effect. *Cyberpsychology and Behaviour, 7*(3), 321-26.

21 **Valkenburg, P.M., Peter, J. & Schouten, A.P.** (2006). Friend networking sites and their relationship to

adolescents; well-being and social self-esteem. *Cyberpsychology & Behaviour, 9*(5), 584-90.

22 **Best, P., Manktelow, R. & Taylor, B.J.** (2014). Online communication, social networking and adolescent wellbeing: a systemic narrative review. *Children and Youth Services Review. 41*, 27-36.

23 **Jelenchick, Eickhoff & Moreno** (2012). "Facebook Depression?" Social networking site use and depression in older adolescents. *Journal of Adolescent Health, 7*, 128-30.

24 **Woods, H.C. and Scott, H.** (2016). #Sleepyteens: social media use in adolescence is associated with poor sleep quality, anxiety, depression and low self-esteem. *Journal of Adolescence, 51*, 41-49.

25 **Bonetti,L., Campbell, M.A.,& Gilmore, L.** (2010). The relationship of loneliness and social anxiety with children's and adolescents' online communication. Queensland University of Technology.

26 **Harman, J.P., Hansen, C.E., Cochran, M.E. & Lindsey, C.R.** (2005). Liar, Liar: Internet faking but not frequency of use affects social skills, self-esteem, social anxiety and aggression. *Cyberpsychology and Behaviour, 8*(1), 1–6.

27 **Meier, E.P., & Gray, J.** (2014) Facebook photo activity associated with body image disturbance in adolescent girls. *Cyberpsychology, Behavior and Social Networking 17*(4), 199-206.

28 www.ditchthelabel.org/wp-content/uploads/2017/07/The-Annual-Bullying-Survey-2017-1.pdf

29 **Kardaras, N.** (2017). *Glow Kids,* St Martin's Griffin: New York

30 **Kardaras, N.** (2017). *Glow Kids,* St Martin's Griffin: New York

31 www.commonsensemedia.org/about-us/news/press-releases/new-report-finds-teens-feel-addicted-to-their-phones-causing-tension-at

32 Thornton, B., Faires, A., Robbins, M., & Rollins, E. (2014). The mere presence of a cell phone may be distracting: Implications for attention and task performance. *Social Psychology, 45*(6), 479-88.

USEFUL WEBSITES

If you are experiencing any concerns about your safety or wellbeing online, your first point of call should be to a parent, carer or trusted adult, who will be able to help you. But if you want or need further advice or guidance, the below web pages are great places to start. Please note that this is not an exhaustive list, and every country will have its own resources and services, so do seek further guidance if you need to.

UK and Ireland

www.saferinternet.org.uk

www.childnet.com

www.bullying.co.uk

www.internetmatters.org

www.stopspeaksupport.com

www.antibullyingpro.com/support-centre

www.nationalbullyinghelpline.co.uk

www.childline.org.uk

www.nspcc.org.uk

www.iwf.org.uk (The Internet Watch Foundation)

stopitnow.org.uk

www.ditchthelabel.org

US and North America:

Stopbullying.gov

Connectsafely.org

STOMPoutbullying.org

Send This Instead – a Canadian app with comebacks for requests of sexting.

www.cybercivilrights.org

the *Shaw* **mind**
FOUNDATION

Creating hope for children,
adults and families

Sign up to our charity, The Shaw Mind Foundation

www.shawmindfoundation.org

and keep in touch with us; we would love to hear
from you.

Our goal is to make help and support available for every
single person in society, from all walks of life.
We will never stop offering hope. These are our promises.

www.triggerpublishing.com

Trigger is a publishing house devoted to opening conversations about mental health. We tell the stories of people who have suffered from mental illnesses and recovered, so that others may learn from them.

Adam Shaw is a worldwide mental health advocate and philanthropist. Now in recovery from mental health issues, he is committed to helping others suffering from debilitating mental health issues through the global charity he co-founded, The Shaw Mind Foundation. www.shawmindfoundation.org

Lauren Callaghan (CPsychol, PGDipClinPsych, PgCert, MA (hons), LLB (hons), BA), born and educated in New Zealand, is an innovative industry-leading psychologist based in London, United Kingdom. Lauren has worked with children and young people, and their families, in a number of clinical settings providing evidence based treatments for a range of illnesses, including anxiety and obsessional problems. She was a psychologist at the specialist national treatment centres for severe obsessional problems in the UK and is renowned as an expert in the field of mental health, recognised for diagnosing and successfully treating OCD and anxiety related illnesses in particular. In addition to appearing as a treating clinician in the critically acclaimed and BAFTA award-winning documentary *Bedlam*, Lauren is a frequent guest speaker on mental health conditions in the media and at academic conferences. Lauren also acts as a guest lecturer and honorary researcher at the Institute of Psychiatry Kings College, UCL.

Please visit the link below:

www.triggerpublishing.com

Join us and follow us...

@triggerpub
@Shaw_Mind

Search for us on Facebook